GIFTED AND TALENTED TEST PREPARATION

NNAT®2 WORKBOOK
FOR AGES 4-6

2016 EDITION

Written and Published by
Origins Tutoring

Printed in the United States of America

First Printing, 2016

ISBN: 978-0-9977680-0-8

The second edition of the Naglieri Nonverbal Ability Test® (NNAT®2) is a registered trademark of NCS Pearson Inc., which is not affiliated with Origins Tutoring. NCS Pearson Inc. has not endorsed the contents of this book.

Origins Tutoring
New York, NY, USA

Email:info@originstutoring.com
www.originstutoring.com

BONUS NNAT®2 PRACTICE TEST

Don't forget to download our bonus
NNAT®2 practice test online to help your child prepare for the actual
NNAT®2 test.

The bonus practice test is available on our website.

Please visit **www.originstutoring.com/bonus-test-7** to acccss the bonus test.

This online test will help your child get used to the different materials
presented on the NNAT®2 and become more familiarized with the process of
taking a standardized test.

We recommend you go through this workbook with your child first and then
have your child take the NNAT®2 practice test at
www.originstutoring.com/bonus-test-7

Table of Contents

About Origins Tutoring

Origins Tutoring helps students develop their higher-order thinking skills while also improving their chances of admission into gifted and accelerated-learner programs.

Our goal is to unleash and nurture the genius in every student. We do this by offering educational and test prep services and materials that are fun, challenging, and provide a sense of accomplishment.

Please contact us with any questions.

info@originstutoring.com
www.originstutoring.com

The Naglieri Nonverbal Ability Test® (NNAT®)

Overview

The second edition of the Naglieri Nonverbal Ability Test (NNAT®2) is designed to assess the cognitive skills that relate to academic success in school for students between four and 18.

The questions on the NNAT®2 consist of geometric figures, shapes, and symbols. A child must use visual reasoning and logical thinking to decipher the answers. The test does not require a child to be able to read, write or speak in the English Language.

The NNAT®2 has 48 multiple-choice questions and offers both an online version and a paper and pencil test. It takes approximately 30 minutes to complete.

The second edition of the Naglieri Nonverbal Ability Test – the NNAT®2 - is used as a 'gifted and talented test' to identify children from diverse linguistic and cultural populations for gifted programs across the USA. It is also used as a placement test in school settings to assess whether a child would benefit from advanced or remedial classes.

How to Use this Book

The NNAT®2 is an important test and the more your child is familiar with the questions on the exam, the better she or he will fare when taking the test.

This workbook will help your child get used to the format and content of the test so she will be adequately prepared and feel confident on test day.

In this workbook, you'll find:

- **93** skill-builder exercises to help your child improve the logical and visual reasoning skills required for excelling on the test.

- **108** NNAT®2 practice questions with answer keys covering all four question types found on the exam.

- Detailed descriptions of question types.

- Teaching tips to help your child approach each test type strategically and with confidence.

- Access to additional bonus **online** NNAT®2 practice test.

Please note that the questions on the official NNAT® test have only two colors: blue and yellow. In this workbook, we use multiple colors to keep your child interested as he or she progresses through the book.

We suggest you begin by helping your child go through the skill-building exercises in Part II of the book. These exercises provide an opportunity for students to learn the concepts and strengthen the fundamental skills required to successfully tackle questions on the official exam.

The skill-building activities are followed by over one hundred NNAT®2 practice questions, divided into sections based on the four question types found on the NNAT®2. Please use the teaching tips provided at the beginning of each of these sections to guide your child as he or she progresses through the questions.

Test Prep Tips and Strategies

Firstly, and most importantly, commit to making the test preparation process a stress-free one. Helping your child keep calm and focused in the face of challenge is a quality that will benefit him throughout his academic life.

Be prepared for difficult questions from the get-go! There will be a certain percentage of questions that are very challenging for all kids. It is key to encourage your child to use all strategies available to him or her when faced with challenging questions. And remember that your kid can get quite a few questions wrong and still do very well on the test.

These additional strategies may also be useful as you help your child prepare:

Before You Start

- Find a quiet, comfortable spot to work free of distractions.

- Tell your child you will be doing some fun activities together.

- Show your child how to perform the simple technique of shading (and erasing) bubbles. If your child is in pre-K, she will only have to point at the correct answer.

During Prep

- If your child is challenged by a question, **ask** your child to **explain why** he or she chose a specific answer. If the answer was incorrect, this will help you identify where your child is stumbling. If the answer was correct, asking your child to articulate her reasoning aloud will help reinforce the concept.

- Encourage your child to carefully **consider all the answer options** before selecting one.

- If your child is stumped by a question, she or he can use the **process of elimination**. First, encourage your child to eliminate obviously wrong answers to narrow down the answer choices. If your child is still in doubt after using this technique, tell him or her to guess as there are no points deducted for wrong answers.

- Encourage your child to visualise the correct answer in the empty box before checking the answer options.

When to Start Preparing?

Every family and student will approach preparation for this test differently. There is no 'right' way to prepare; there is only the best way for a particular child and family.

We suggest students, at minimum, take one full-length practice test and spend 6-8 hours working through NNAT®2 type practice questions.

If you have limited time to prepare, spend most energy reviewing areas where your child is encountering the majority of problems.

As they say, knowledge is power! Preparing for the NNAT®2 test will certainly help your child avoid anxiety and make sure she does not give up too soon when faced with unfamiliar and perplexing questions.

Skill-building Exercises

The skill-building exercises are divided into five sections:

What Does Not Belong

Connecting and Taking Apart Shapes

Patterns and Puzzles

Repeating Patterns

Sequences

These exercises were designed to help your child learn the concepts and strengthen the fundamental skills required to successfully tackle questions on the official NNAT®2 test.

The activities will help develop your child's ability to identify:
- differences in visual figures and shapes;
- how shapes and figures appear when combined or separated;
- how a shape and/or figure transforms by sliding, flipping, or rotating;
- when a shape or figure repeats to complete a pattern; and
- how shapes and figures progress sequentially according to a rule.

What Does Not Belong

This skill-building section helps your child develop his or her ability to identify differences in visual figures and shapes.

In the "What Does Not Belong" exercises, ask your child to identify which of the five pictures does not belong with the others in the row.

Example:

①   ②   ③   ④   ⑤

Explanation: In the row above, there are five pictures. The one that does not belong with the others is option choice 4. In this picture, the pink arrow inside the blue circle is pointing downwards. In the other pictures, the pink arrow is pointing to the side.

Which shape does not belong with others?

1

    ①   ②   ③   ④   ⑤

2

    ①   ②   ③   ④   ⑤

3

    ①   ②   ③   ④   ⑤

4

    ①   ②   ③   ④   ⑤

5

    ①   ②   ③   ④   ⑤

Which shape does not belong with others?

6

       (1)   (2)   (3)   (4)   (5)

7

       (1)   (2)   (3)   (4)   (5)

8

       (1)   (2)   (3)   (4)   (5)

9

       (1)   (2)   (3)   (4)   (5)

10

       (1)   (2)   (3)   (4)   (5)

Which shape does not belong with others?

11

① ② ③ ④ ⑤

12

① ② ③ ④ ⑤

13

① ② ③ ④ ⑤

14

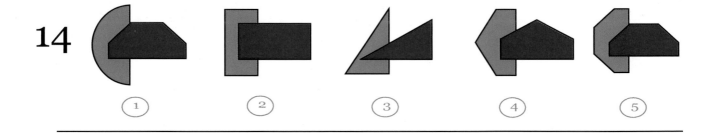

① ② ③ ④ ⑤

15

① ② ③ ④ ⑤

Connecting & Taking Apart Shapes

This skill-building section helps your child develop his or her ability to identify differences in visual figures and shapes, and how shapes and figures appear when combined or separated.

In the first exercises (**Connecting Shapes**), ask your child to identify what the two shapes at the beginning of the row would look like when they are connected together.

Example:

Explanation: At the beginning of row above, there are two curved shapes, one yellow and one red. When these two shapes are connected, they create the shape in option one, which is the correct answer.

In the second exercises (**Taking Apart Shapes**), ask your child to look at the shape at the beginning of the row and identify the two shapes it would become if taken apart. In this exercise, your child must choose two answers.

Example:

Explanation: At the beginning of row above is a shape with a blue piece and a grey piece. When taken apart, this shape becomes the blue figure in option one and the grey figure in option three, which are the correct answers.

Which shape is created when the first two shapes are connected together?

1 ◀ + ▶ = ⬟① 🦋② 🦋③ ⬟④

2 ◖ + ◗ = ①②③④

3 ◖ + ◗ = ①②③④

4 ✦ + ➤ = ★①②③④

5 | + ■ = ①②③④

Which shape is created when the first two shapes are connected together?

6

⬜ + ◼ = ① ② ③ ④

7

⬠ + ◢ = ① ② ③ ④

8

▲ + ▽ = ① ② ③ ④

9

⬛ + ◻ = ① ② ③ ④

10

▷ + ◀ = ① ② ③ ④

Which shape is created when the first two shapes are connected together?

11

12

13

14

15

Which two shapes are created when the first shape is taken apart?

1 =

①   ②   ③   ④

2  =

①   ②   ③   ④

3 =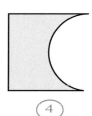

①   ②   ③   ④

4 =

①   ②   ③   ④

5

①   ②   ③   ④

Which two shapes are created when the first shape is taken apart?

6 =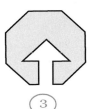

                                           ①   ②   ③   ④

7 =

                                           ①   ②   ③   ④

8  =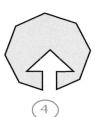

                                           ①   ②   ③   ④

9 = 

                                           ①   ②   ③   ④

10 =

                                           ①   ②   ③   ④

Which two shapes are created when the first shape is taken apart?

11 =

         ①   ②   ③   ④

12  =

         ①   ②   ③   ④

13 =

         ①   ②   ③   ④

14 =

         ①   ②   ③   ④

15 =

         ①   ②   ③   ④

Puzzles and Patterns

These skill-builder activities help your child develop the skills needed to successfully tackle the pattern completion section on the NNAT2.

In the first exercises (**Finding Puzzle Piece**), ask your child to identify, among the answer options, the missing puzzle piece that exactly completes the missing piece of the patterned square at the beginning of the row.

Example:

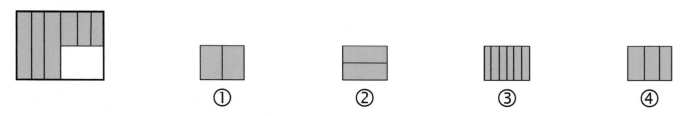

Explanation: At the beginning of the row above is a blue square with vertical black stripes. The picture among the answer options that completes the pattern is option 4, as this 'puzzle piece' would match the stripes exactly if placed into the empty square.

In the second exercises (**Matching Patterns**), ask your child to identify which of the patterns in the answer options matches exactly the pattern presented at the beginning of the row.

Example:

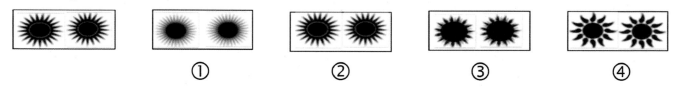

Explanation: At the beginning of row above is a rectangle with black suns. The pattern that matches this initial pattern exactly is shown in answer option 2.

Which piece fits in the white square to complete the puz

1 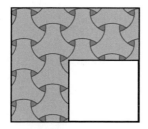 =
① ② ③ ④

2 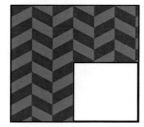 =
① ② ③ ④

3  =
① ② ③ ④

4 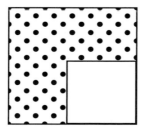 =
① ② ③ ④

5  =
① ② ③ ④

Which piece fits in the white square to complete the puzzle?

6 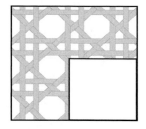 =
① ② ③ ④

7  =
① ② ③ ④

8 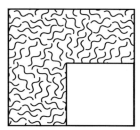 =
① ② ③ ④

9 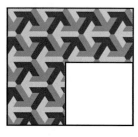 =
① ② ③ ④

10 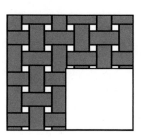 =
① ② ③ ④

Which piece fits in the white square to complete the puzzle?

11  =
   ① ② ③ ④

12 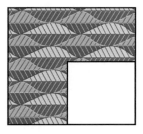 =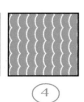
   ① ② ③ ④

13 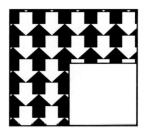 =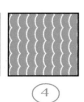
   ① ② ③ ④

14 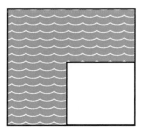 = ① ② ③ ④

15 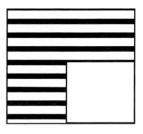 =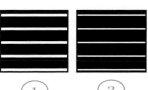
   ① ② ③ ④

Which pattern matches the pattern at the beginning of the row?

1   =

② ② ③ ④

2   =

① ② ③ ④

3   =

① ② ③ ④

4   =

① ② ③ ④

5   =

① ② ③ ④

Which pattern matches the pattern at the beginning of the row?

6

① ② ③ ④

7

① ② ③ ④

8

① ② ③ ④

9

① ② ③ ④

10

① ② ③ ④

Which pattern matches the pattern at the beginning of the row?

11 =

①　　②　　③　　④

12 =

①　　②　　③　　④

13 =

①　　②　　③　　④

14  =

①　　②　　③　　④

15 =

①　　②　　③　　④

Repeating Patterns

This skill-builder section helps your child develop his or her ability to identify when a shape or a figure repeats to complete a pattern.

In these exercises, ask your child to identify which picture among the answer options comes next in the pattern.

Example:

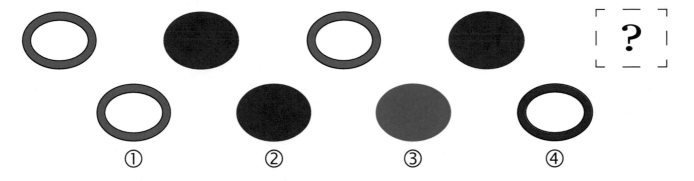

① ② ③ ④

Explanation: The first row above shows a pattern that alternates between a green/white circle, and a pink circle. The shape among the answer options that would continue this pattern is the green/white circle, which is answer option 1.

Which picture completes the pattern in the first row?

1

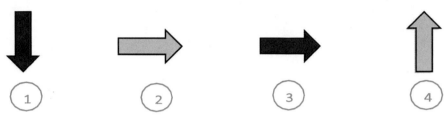

① ② ③ ④

2

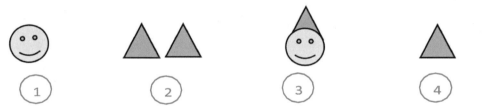

① ② ③ ④

3

① ② ③ ④

Which picture completes the pattern in the first row?

4    

   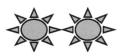

①   ②   ③   ④

5

①   ②   ③   ④

6

①   ②   ③   ④

Which picture completes the pattern in the first row?

7

(1)   (2)   (3)   (4)

8

(1)   (2)   (3)   (4)

9

(1)   (2)   (3)   (4)

Sequences

These skill-building activities help your child develop his or her ability to identify how a shape transforms by sliding, flipping, or rotating, and how a shape progresses sequentially according to a rule.

In these exercises, ask your child to look at the first row of pictures and identify which picture in the second row would come next in the sequence (i.e: the picture that would best go in the place represented by the question mark box).

Example:

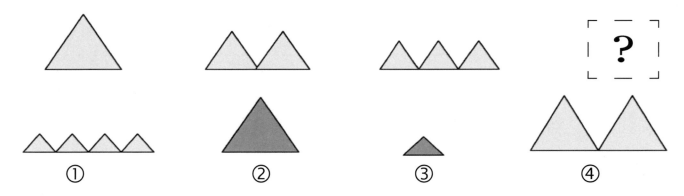

Explanation: In the first row above, the first picture is of one large yellow triangle followed by two smaller yellow triangles in the second picture. The third picture shows three even smaller yellow triangles. The next picture in the series should therefore follows the rule of the sequence which is that each triangle adds an additional one *and* gets smaller as the sequence progresses. Therefore, the correct answer is option 1 (four yellow triangles that are smaller than the three preceding triangles).

Which object in the second row comes next in the sequence?

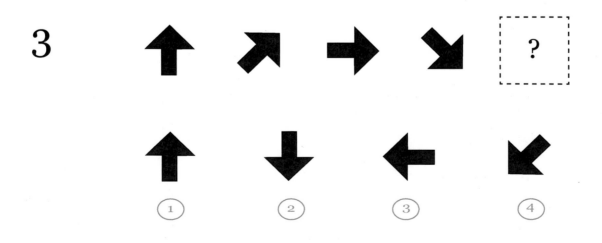

NNAT®2 Test Prep Workbook   © Origins Tutoring Inc.

Which object in the second row comes next in the sequence?

4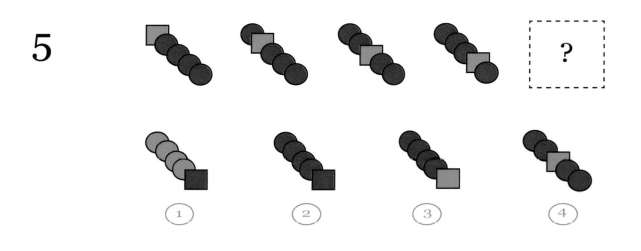

5

6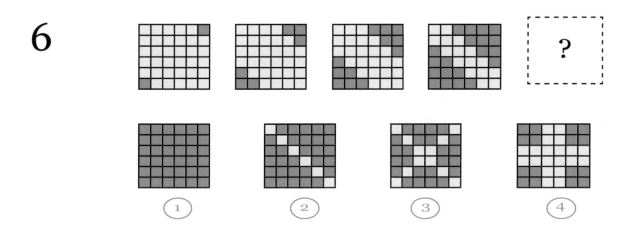

Which object in the second row comes next in the sequence?

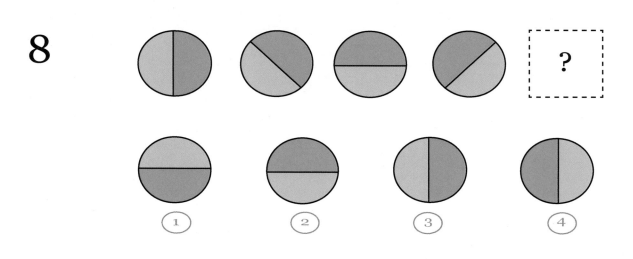

NNAT®2 Practice Questions

The NNAT®2 is comprised of four main 'question' types. The following four sections provide practice questions on each of these four question types.

Pattern Completion

Reasoning by Analogy

Serial Reasoning

Spatial Visualization

Each question type involves the following steps:

- The student is presented with a picture of a matrix.

- The student must observe and detect the relationship among the parts of the matrix.

- The student must solve the problem based on the information shown to her within the matrix, and choose the correct answer from five possible options.

Before your child attempts the practice questions, spend a few minutes yourself reviewing the teaching tips for each section so you can be prepared to help your child if he or she struggles with a question.

The NNAT®2 practice questions will help your child use and bolster the skills needed to succeed on the actual test. As you watch your child tackle the practice questions, you will also be able to identify the question types that your child finds most challenging and provide extra practice for him or her in those areas.

Remember to download a bonus NNAT®2 practice test at www.originstutoring.com/bonus-test-7

Pattern Completion

With this question type, the child is presented with a design in a rectangle. Inside the large rectangle is a smaller white rectangle representing a missing piece that completes the design. The child must choose the answer that best fits the inner rectangle so that the missing parts complete the design.

These questions are the most common question types found on the Level A and B tests, and are the easiest kinds of matrices in the exam.

Before each question in this section, say to your child:

"Look at the picture. A piece is missing where you see the question mark. Show me the piece that is missing in the answer choices."

After a few questions, your child will probably not need this prompt and will spontaneously point to or mark an answer.

Tips and Strategies

Ask your student to complete the picture by continuing the correct lines and colors of the design into the empty box. Then, match the drawing with the correct answer choice.

Ask your student to note the color and design next to the corners of the empty box as this is a useful base to help identify the correct answer.

Go through each answer option and ask the student to visualize how each choice would fit the design.

1

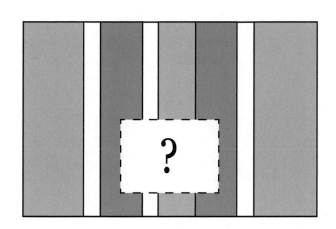

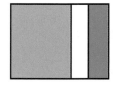 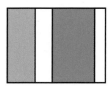 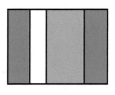 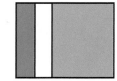 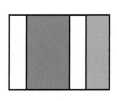

①　　②　　③　　④　　⑤

2

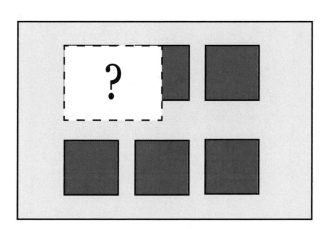

 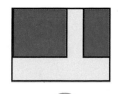 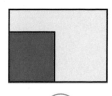 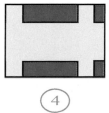 

①　　②　　③　　④　　⑤

　　NNAT®2 Test Prep Workbook

3

  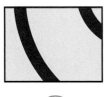 

1   2   3   4   5

4

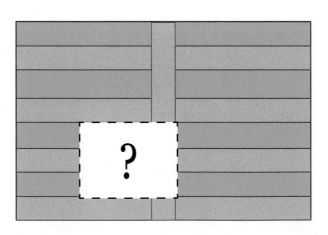

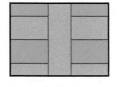  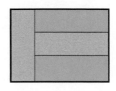 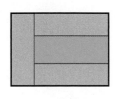 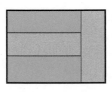

1   2   3   4   5

5

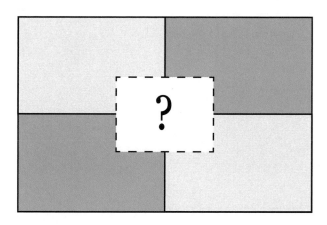

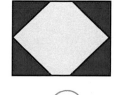 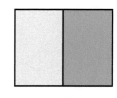 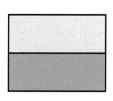 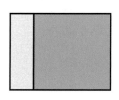 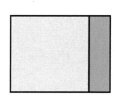

①   ②   ③   ④   ⑤

6

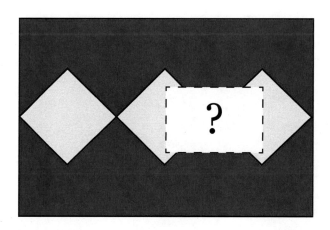

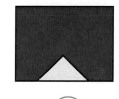   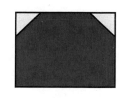

①   ②   ③   ④   ⑤

7

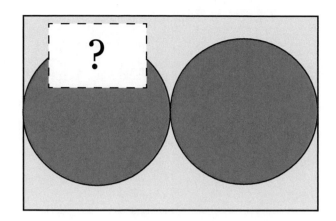

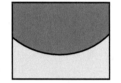 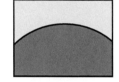 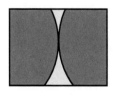 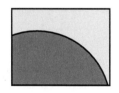 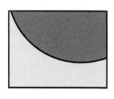

①   ②   ③   ④   ⑤

8

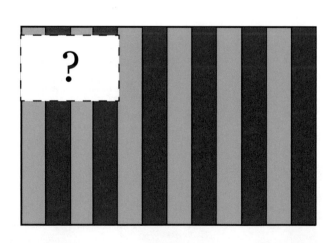

①   ②   ③   ④   ⑤

9

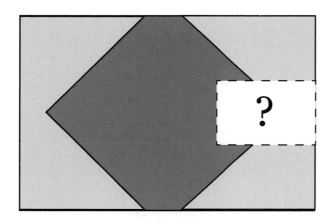

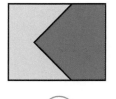 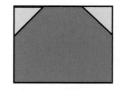 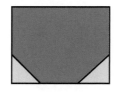 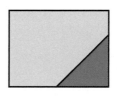 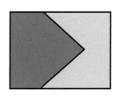

① ② ③ ④ ⑤

10

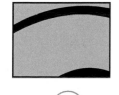    

① ② ③ ④ ⑤

11

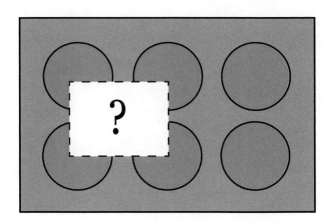

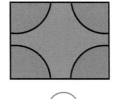 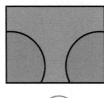 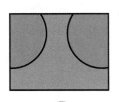 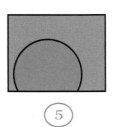 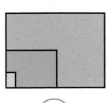

   (1)   (2)   (3)   (4)   (5)

12

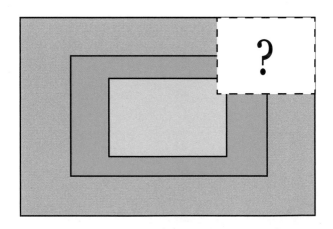

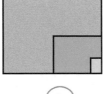 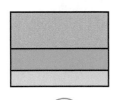 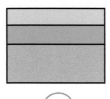 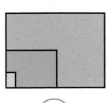 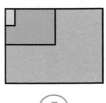

   (1)   (2)   (3)   (4)   (5)

13

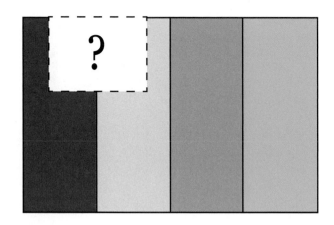

 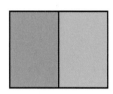  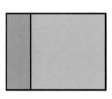

① ② ③ ④ ⑤

14

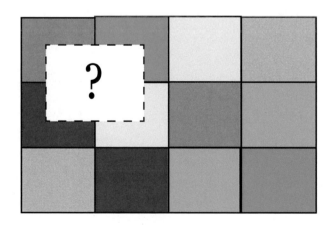

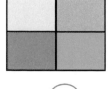 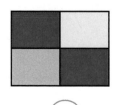 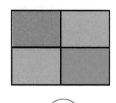 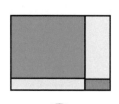 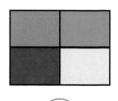

① ② ③ ④ ⑤

NNAT®2 Test Prep Workbook

15

①   ②   ③   ④   ⑤

16

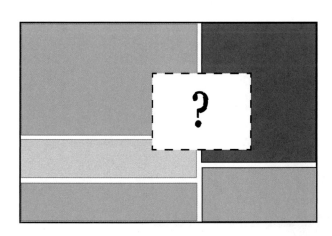

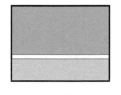 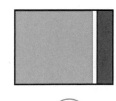 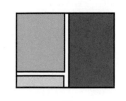  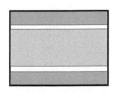

①   ②   ③   ④   ⑤

17

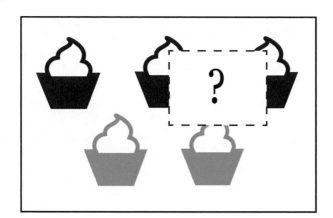

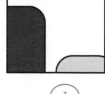    

① ② ③ ④ ⑤

18

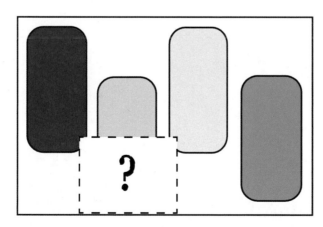

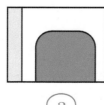 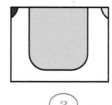 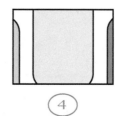 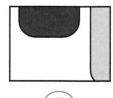

① ② ③ ④ ⑤

19

      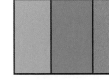   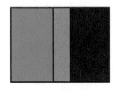   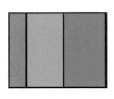

①   ②   ③   ④   ⑤

20

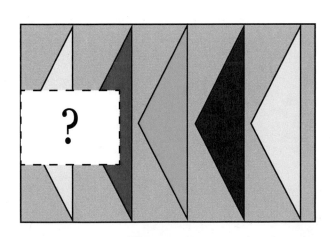

   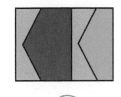   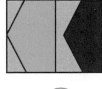   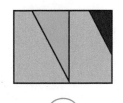   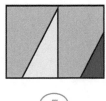

①   ②   ③   ④   ⑤

21

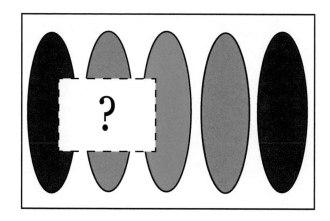

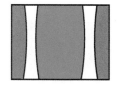 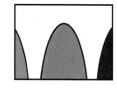 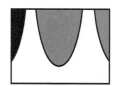 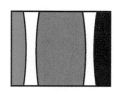 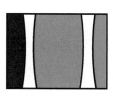

①   ②   ③   ④   ⑤

22

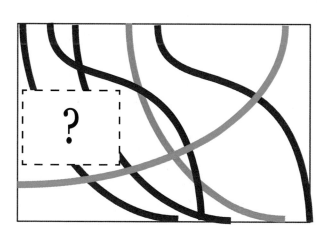

   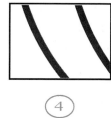 

①   ②   ③   ④   ⑤

23

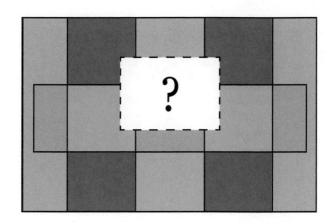

   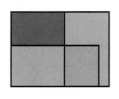 

①　　　②　　　③　　　④　　　⑤

24

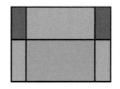  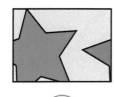 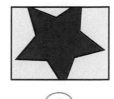

①　　　②　　　③　　　④　　　⑤

25

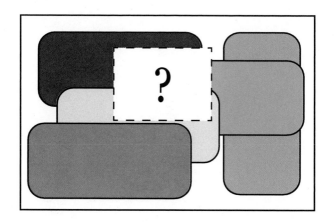

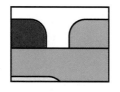

(1)

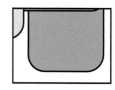

(2)

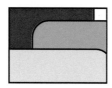

(3)

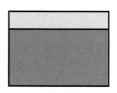

(4)

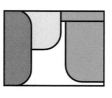

(5)

26

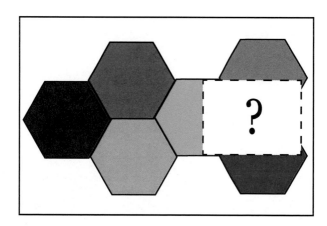

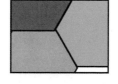

(1)

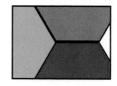

(2)

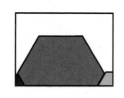

(3)

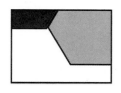

(4)

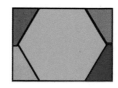

(5)

27

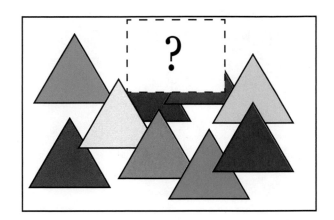

         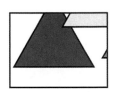

①   ②   ③   ④   ⑤

28

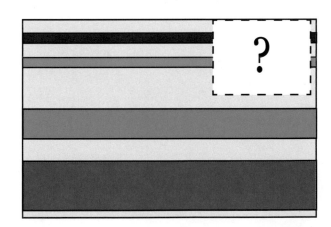

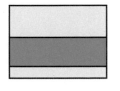   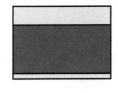      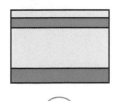   

①   ②   ③   ④   ⑤

29

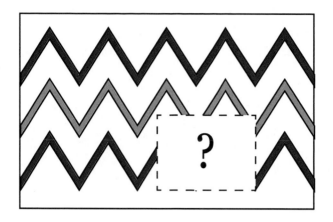

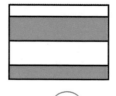

① ② ③ ④ ⑤

30

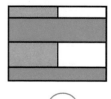
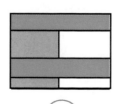
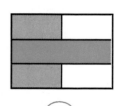
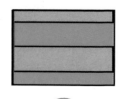

① ② ③ ④ ⑤

31

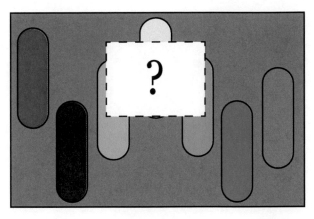

Yes

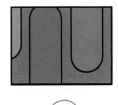 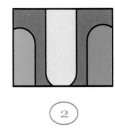 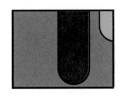 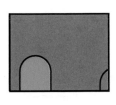 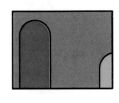

| 1 | 2 | 3 | 4 | 5 |

32

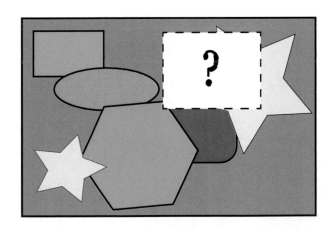

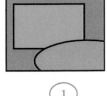 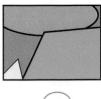 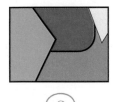 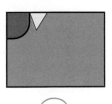 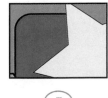

| 1 | 2 | 3 | 4 | 5 |

33

①   ②   ③   ④   ⑤

34

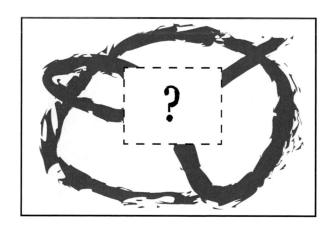

①   ②   ③   ④   ⑤

35

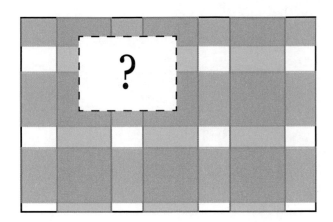

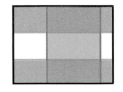  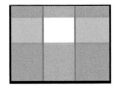 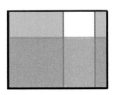 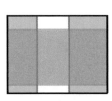

1   2   3   4   5

36

  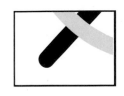 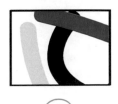 

1   2   3   4   5

Reasoning by Analogy

With this question type, the child is presented with a matrix of 4-6 boxes containing objects, usually geometric shapes.

To solve the problem, the child must determine how the object changes as it moves across the row and down the column in the matrix. The question may require that the student pay close attention to several aspects of the design (e.g: shading, color, shape) at the same time.

Before each question in this section, say to your child:

"Look at the picture. A piece is missing where you see the question mark. Show me the piece that is missing in the answer choices."

Tips and Strategies

Make sure your student knows key concepts that come up in these types of questions, including geometric concepts such as rotational symmetry, line symmetry, parts of a whole.

If your student is finding these items difficult, encourage her to discover the pattern by looking in each direction (horizontally and vertically).

- Ask: "How do the objects change in the first row? Do you see a pattern? Do the objects change in the same way in the second row? The third row?"

- Ask: "How do the objects change in the first column? Do you see a pattern? Do the objects change in the same way in the second column? The third column?"

Encourage your student to isolate one element (e.g: outer shape, inner shape/s) and identify how it changes:

- Is the color/shading of the element changing as it moves?

- Is the element changing positions as it moves? Does it move up or down? Clockwise or counter-clockwise? Does it end up in the opposite (mirror) position?

- Does the element disappear and appear again as it move along the row/column? Does it get bigger or smaller?

Encourage your student to make a prediction for the missing object and compare the description with the answer choices.

1

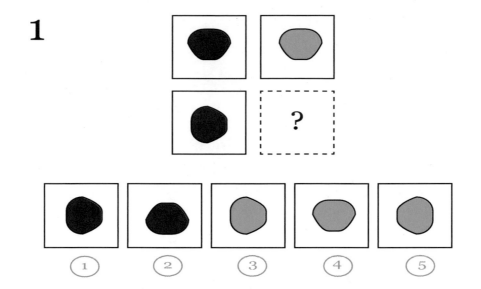

2

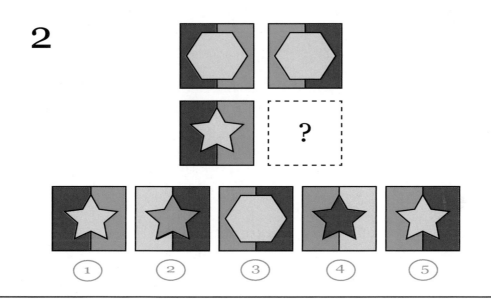

3

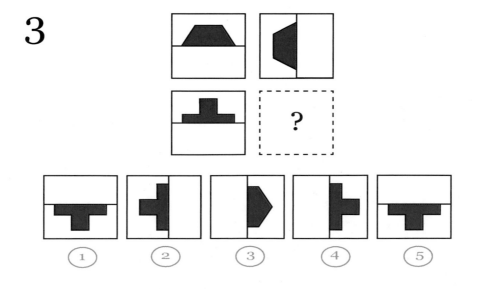

4

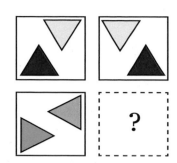

5

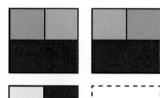

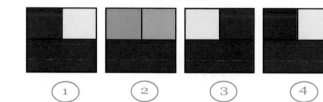

6

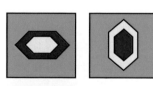

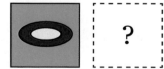

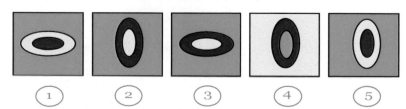

7

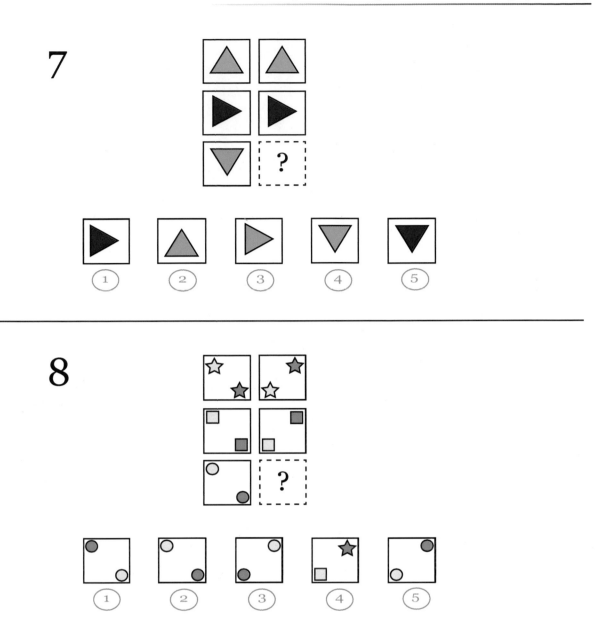

8

9

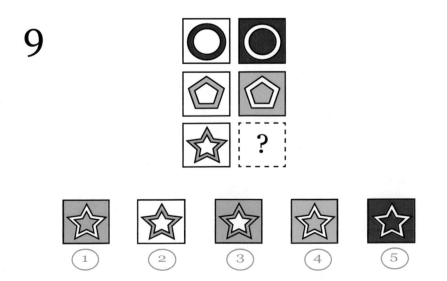

10

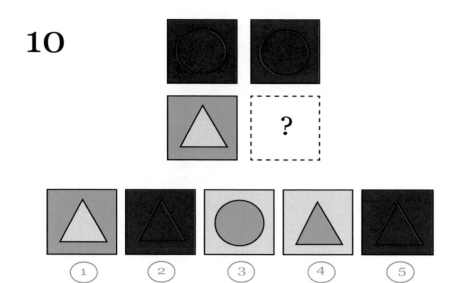

11

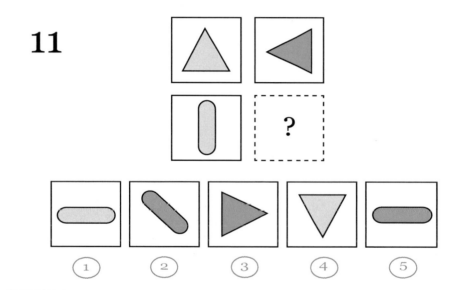

12

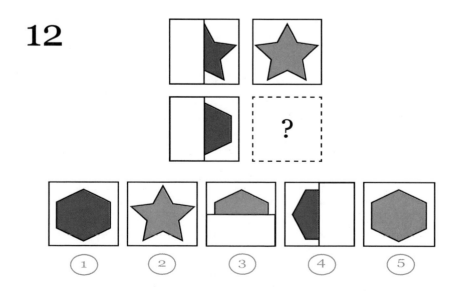

13

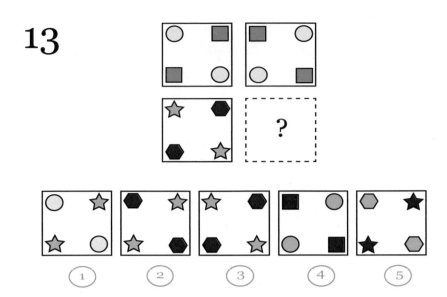

14

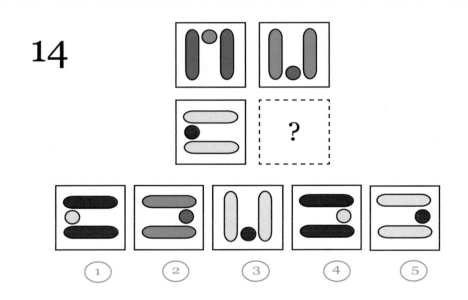

15

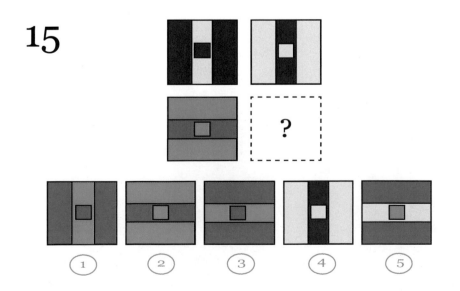

16

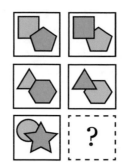

① ② ③ ④ ⑤

17

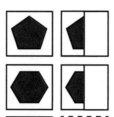

① ② ③ ④ ⑤

18

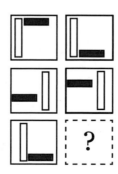

① ② ③ ④ ⑤

19

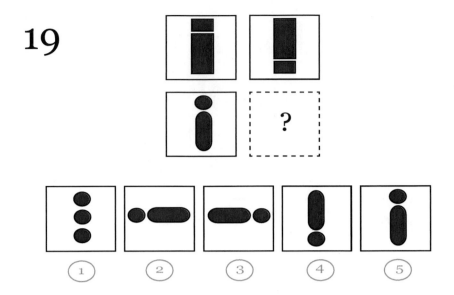

20

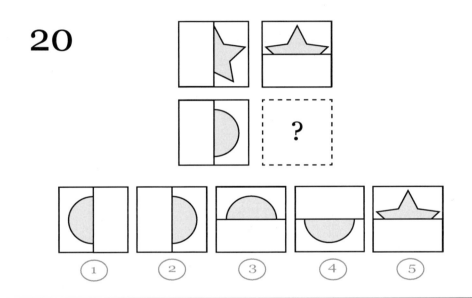

21

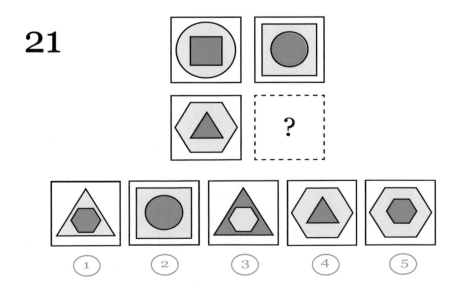

22

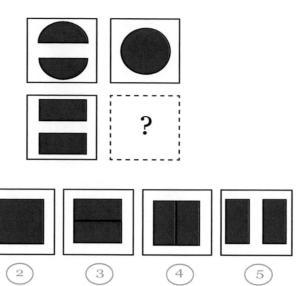

23

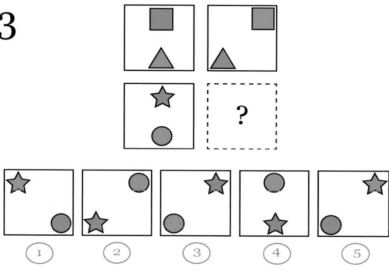

24

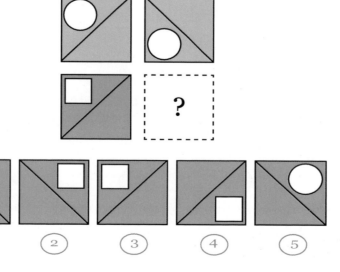

25

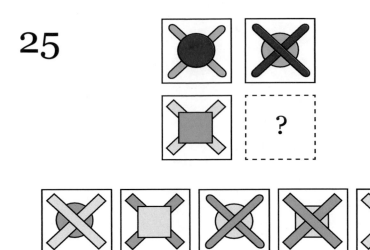

26

27

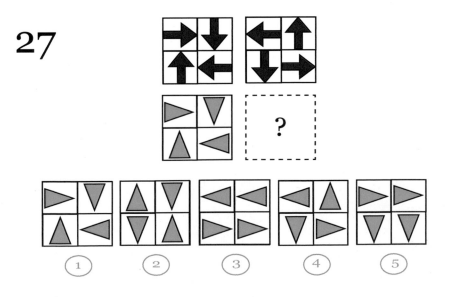

28

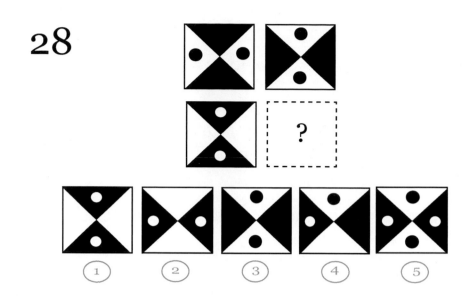

29

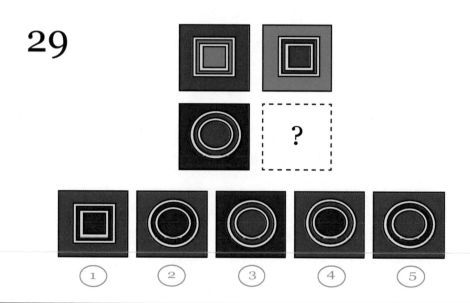

30

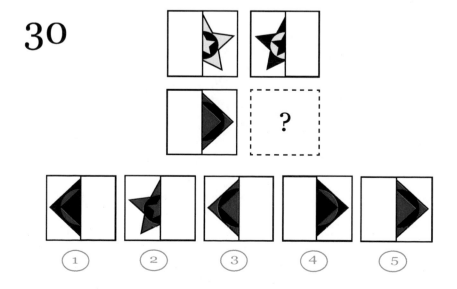

Serial Reasoning

With this question type, the student is shown a series of shapes that change across the rows and columns throughout the design. These questions require the child to understand how the objects in rows and columns relate to each other. The child must isolate and apply the rule/s in order to identify which object from the answer choices fits the empty box in the bottom right-hand corner of the matrix.

Before each question in this section, say to your child:

"Look at the picture. A piece is missing where you see the question mark. Show me the piece that is missing in the answer choices."

Tips and Strategies

Encourage your student to discover the pattern by looking in each direction.

- Horizontally across the rows. Ask: "How do the objects change in the first row? Do you see a pattern? Do the objects change in the same way in the second row? The third row?"

- Vertically down the columns. Ask: "How do the objects change in the first column? Do you see a pattern? Do the objects change in the same way in the second column? The third column?"

- Diagonally (if the item is a 6-box matrix). Ask: "How do the objects change across the diagonal? Do you see a pattern?"

Encourage your student to isolate one element (e.g: outer shape, inner shape/s) and identify how it changes.

- How does the color/shading of the element change as it moves along the row/column?

- Does the element change positions as it moves along the row/column? Does it move up, down or around (i.e.: clockwise, counter-clockwise). Does the element move to the opposite position?

- Does the element get bigger, smaller or stay the same as it moves?

- Does the element disappear and appear again as you move along the row/column?

1

2

3

4

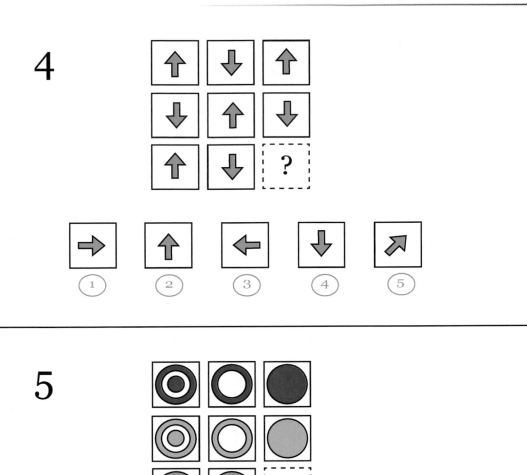

5

6

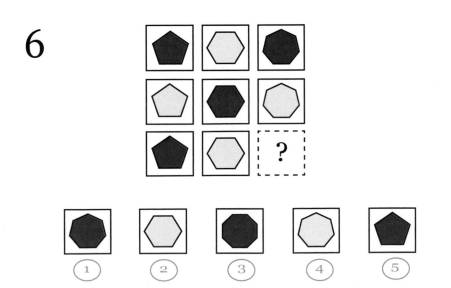

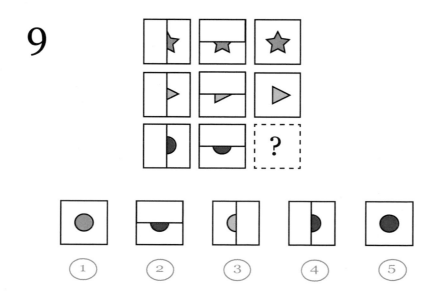

10

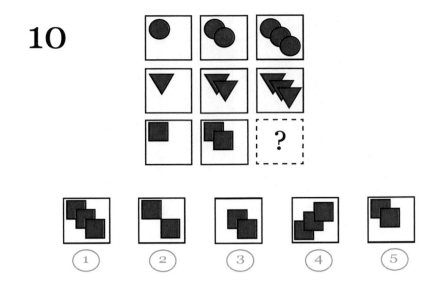

11

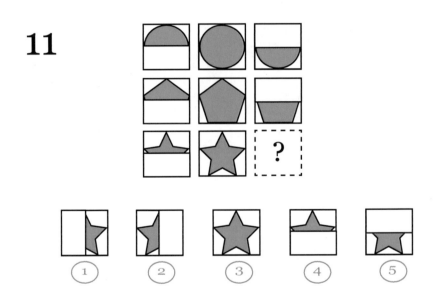

12

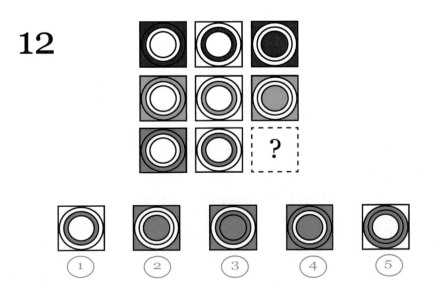

13

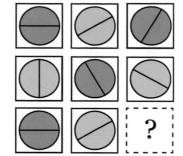

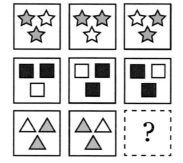

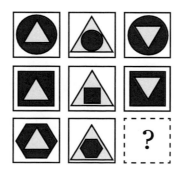

① ② ③ ④ ⑤

14

① ② ③ ④ ⑤

15

① ② ③ ④ ⑤

16

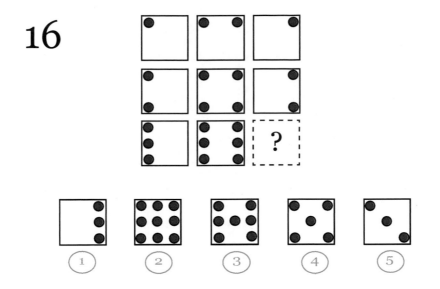

17

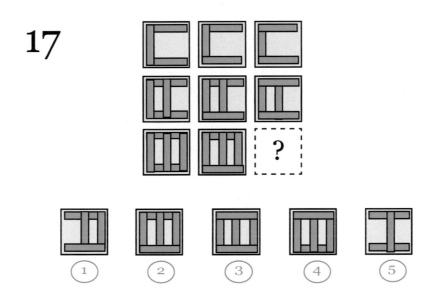

18

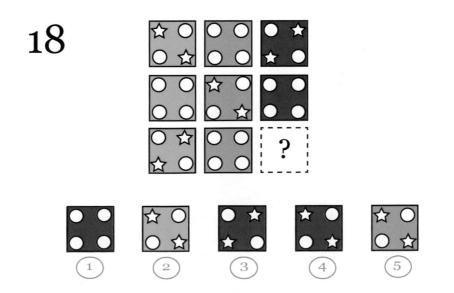

19

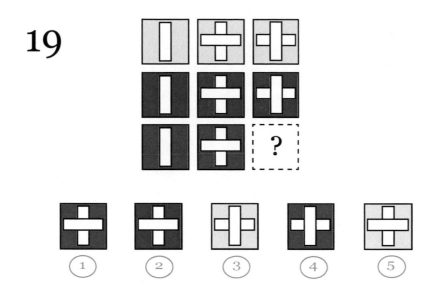

20

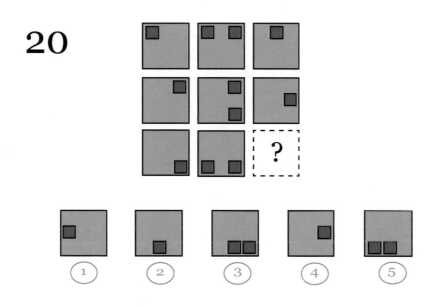

21

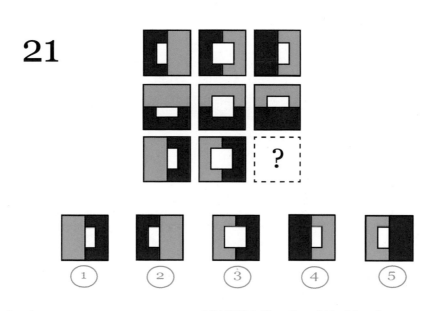

22

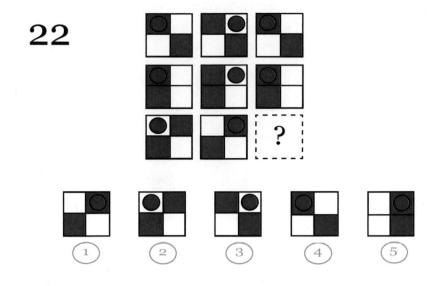

23

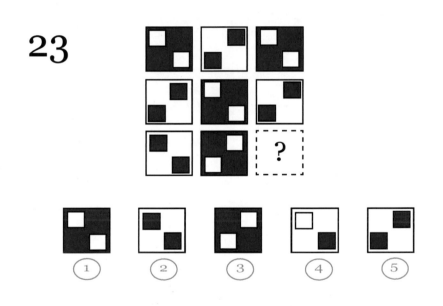

24

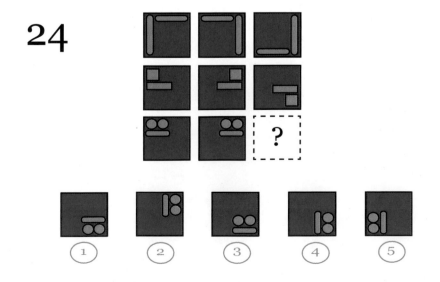

Spatial Visualization

With this question type, a child is presented with a series of objects that combine, invert, transform and/or rotate across rows and columns. The child must identify the rule for the top row of objects and then predict what will happen to objects in the second (or third) row. She must then select which object among the answer choices follows this rule and should go in the empty box in the matrix.

Spatial Visualization items are widely seen to be the most difficult, particularly when involving objects that intersect in ways that are hard to recognize or involve an object rotating.

Before each question in this section, say to your child:

"Look at the picture. A piece is missing where you see the question mark. Show me the piece that is missing in the answer choices."

Tips and Strategies

Ask your student to do some paper-folding projects. This will help her understand how objects on a folded piece of paper appear (and relate to each other) when the paper is opened.

Encourage your student to visualize -- observe, imagine and keep track of -- the changes in the geometric shapes as they move and then draw what she predicts she might see in the empty box.

Encourage your student to isolate one element (e.g: outer shape, inner shape/s) and identify how it changes.

- How does the color/shading of the element change as it moves along the row/column?

- Does the element change positions as it moves along the row/column? Does the element move to the opposite position?

- Does the element flip positions (e.g.: outer square becomes inner square or vice-versa)? Does the element go upside down?

- Does the element combine with another element?

1

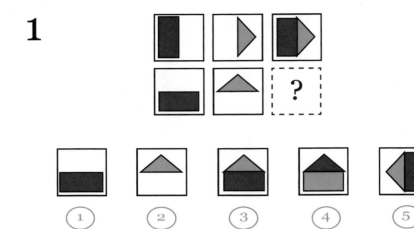

2

3

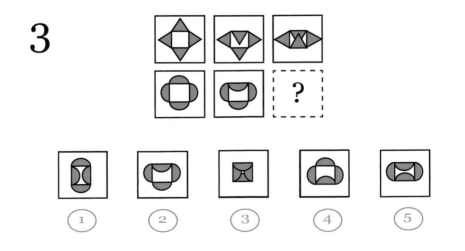

4

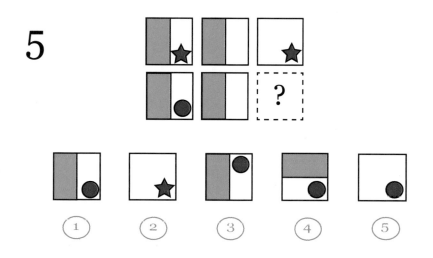

5

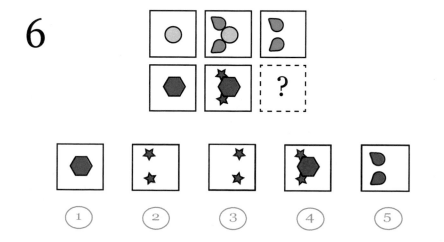

6

7

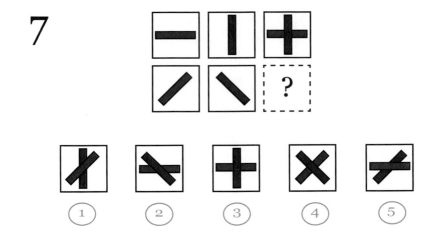

8

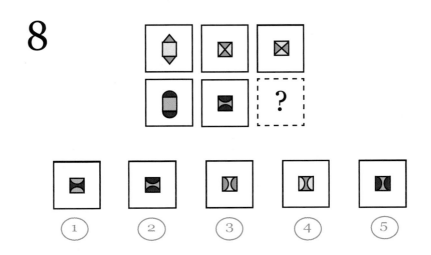

9

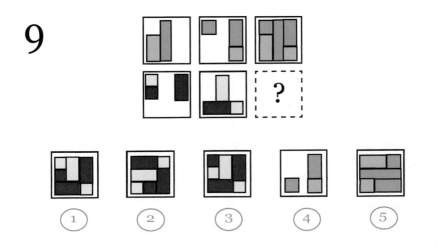

10

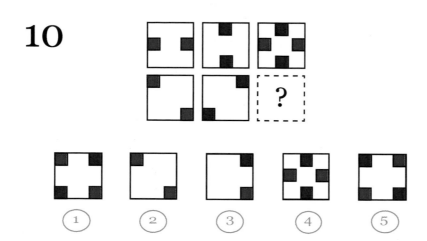

11

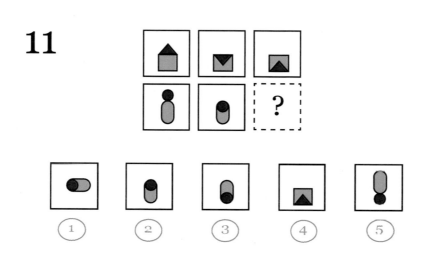

12

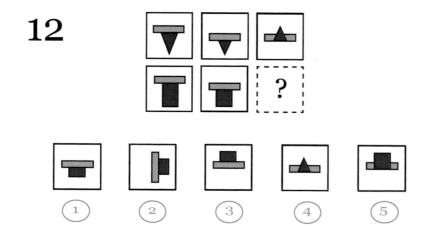

13

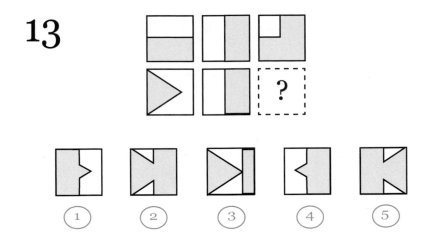

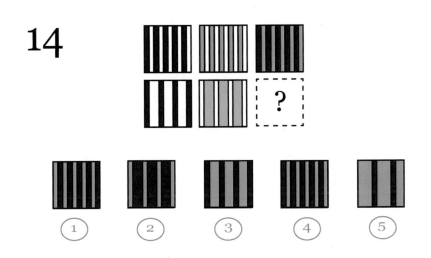

14

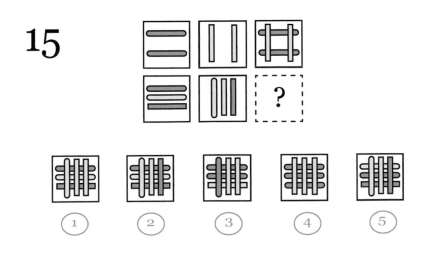

15

16

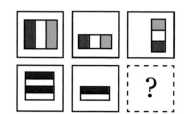

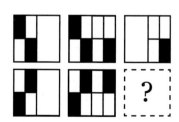

17

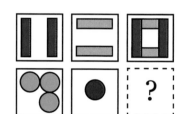

18

Answer Keys
Skill-building Exercises

What Does Not Belong	
What Does Not Belong	
1.	4
2.	2
3.	1
4.	5
5.	2
6.	5
7.	1
8.	3
9.	5
10.	2
11.	4
12.	4
13.	5
14.	1
15.	4

Connecting and Taking Apart Shapes			
Connecting Shapes		Taking Apart Shapes	
1.	1	1.	1 & 4
2.	2	2.	2 & 3
3.	4	3.	2 & 3
4.	3	4.	1 & 2
5.	2	5.	2 & 3
6.	4	6.	3 & 4
7.	1	7.	1 & 4
8.	4	8.	3 & 4
9.	3	9.	1 & 2
10.	3	10.	1 & 3
11.	2	11.	3 & 4
12.	4	12.	1 & 3
13.	1	13.	2 & 3
14.	2	14.	1 & 2
15.	4	15.	1 & 2

Puzzles and Patterns			
Finding a Puzzle Piece		Matching Patterns	
1.	3	1.	2
2.	1	2.	3
3.	3	3.	1
4.	4	4.	3
5.	2	5.	2
6.	2	6.	1
7.	1	7.	2
8.	4	8.	4
9.	3	9.	4
10.	2	10.	3
11.	2	11.	1
12.	4	12.	2
13.	1	13.	3
14.	3	14.	3
15.	4	15.	2

Repeating Patterns	
Repeating Patterns	
1.	2
2.	2
3.	1
4.	4
5.	2
6.	1
7.	3
8.	2
9.	1

Sequences	
Sequences	
1.	4
2.	1
3.	2
4.	2
5.	3
6.	2
7.	1
8.	4
9.	3